THE GATHERING STORM

STORM

MATTHEW 24
The End of the World (Age)
THE COURSE OF THE AGE

BY
Dr. Guy Lee, D.D.

THE GATHERING STORM
by
Dr. Guy Lee, D.D.
37 Bill Presley Road, Cleveland, GA
30528
Phone: 706-865-4555
E-mail: tometterlee@gmail.com
© Guy Lee 2014
May 2020

All Scripture quotations and references
are from
the King James Version of the Holy
Bible.

ISBN 978-1-7347481-5-4

Published by
The Old Paths Publications
www.theoldpathspublications.com
TOP@theoldpathspublications.com
May 2020

TABLE OF CONTENTS

MATTHEW 24

The Gathering Storm

The End of the World (Age)

THE COURSE OF THE AGE

VERSE 1 REMOVING FROM THE TEMPLE

1. *REMOVING FROM THE TEMPLE* - *Verse 1*

   A.   And He went out.

   The nation has rejected its king and the king rejected Israel.

   In Matthew 23:7   Jesus wept over Jerusalem.
   In Verse 38   He says "Behold your house is left unto you desolate.

   In Matthew 21:13   Jesus said "My house shall be called the house of prayer; but ye have made it a den of thieves

In Matthew 23:38 Jesus said "Your house" It is not His house anymore Jesus the God of Israel forsakes His house, "And Jesus went out"

1. When Christ moves out there is desolation and deadness - Matthew 23:38
2. When Christ moves out, the world moves in.
3. When Christian values vanish, worldly values return.
4. When Christian worship ceases, worship of lesser things begin to move in.

VERSE 2 JERUSALEM AND THE TEMPLE WERE DESTROYED BY THE ROMANS IN 70 A.D.

VERSE 3 THE RETURN OF CHRIST INQUIRED

2. *THE RETURN OF CHRIST INQUIRED – Verse 3*

A. Three-fold question

1. When shall these things be?
2. What shall be the sign of thy coming?

7

3. And the end of the world?

- **WHEN SHALL THESE THINGS BE? Verse 3**

OR ... When will Jerusalem and the temple be destroyed?

Answer: **Matthew 24:2**

Fulfilled in 70 A.D. when Jerusalem was destroyed by the Romans.

Daniel 9:26
Luke 21:2024

- **WHAT SHALL BE THE SIGN OF THY COMING? Verse 3**

Answer: **Matthew 24:4-14**

they give: A.   Having a double interpretation

1. The Character of the Age
Wars, International conflicts, pestilences, persecutions and false Christs.

So that these predictions will have a double fulfillment in a

8

lesser degree during the present age of grace and in the coming period of judgment. Then there will be great apostasy when many shall stumble and faithful servants of God will be betrayed by their closest relatives. This too has had a partial fulfillment during this dispensation.

There are 2 stages of the Lord's coming:

1. Rapture
Personal coming in the air, not to the earth, for the church
I Thessalonians 2:19
I Thessalonians 4:13-18

There is an interval of the seven-year tribulation period between the rapture and the Second Advent.

2. Second Advent
Jesus is coming at His second advent with His saints to reign.

Revelation 19:14

9

Paul using the similarity of the Feast of First Fruits which consisted of three parts Leviticus 23:9-12-22, namely:

- THE SHEAF
  Type of Christ's Resurrection - I Corinthians 15:20-23
- THE HARVEST
  The End of the Church Age – I Thessalonians 4:13-18
  Type of the Rapture
- THE GLEANINGS
  The Law of Gleanings – Leviticus 23:22
  Type of the Tribulation Saints

Christ is the First Fruits, I Corinthians 15:20-23 they that are Christ's – the dead in Christ of I Thessalonians 4:16 are the Harvest while those who die during the Tribulation for the witness of Christ make up the Gleanings. All are included in the first resurrection - Revelation 20:4-6. This ends or completes the first resurrection which occurs in more than one stage.

10

- First Stage: Resurrection of the church saints
- Second Stage: Resurrection of the Tribulation saints
            Revelation 20:4-6

There is a seven-year interval between the first and second coming.

- **AND THE END OF THE WORLD? Verse 3**

    OR … What will happen when Jesus comes?

Answer: **Verses 27-331; 40-51; 25:1-46**

We will deal with verses 27-31 & 40-51 when we get to them.

VERSE 4-5 ROAMING FROM THE TRUTH

3. *ROAMING FROM THE TRUTH - Verse 4-5*

    a. **Deception** - Verse 4-5 11-24

    And Jesus answered…."Take heed that no man deceive you."

Deceive means to seduce; to lead astray, to roam.

Multitudes are being deceived by:

11

i.   Seducing Spirits   I
     Timothy 4:1
ii. Doctrines of Devils   I
     Timothy 4:1
iii. Lies   I
     Timothy 4:2
iv. Hypocrisy   I
     Timothy 4:2

Deception is the enemy of all true doctrine.

- It can be self-inflicted
  a. Proverbs 14:12; 21:2; 11:19; I John 1:8
- It can be brought by others
  a. Romans 16:18; Ephesians 4:14; II Thessalonians 2:2-3
- And by Satan himself
  a. Revelation 20:3-8-10

We can "take heed" by knowing the truth in detail. Jesus said "And ye shall know the truth and the truth shall make you free" John 8:32. God's word is true, "Thy word is truth" John 17:17. Jesus is the truth and the only way to heaven, John 14:6; I Timothy 2:5; Acts 4:12.

1. Imposters - Verse 5

There have been many anti-christ's during the church age. John wrote "Even now are there many antichrists: whereby we know that it is the last time. They went out from us, but they were not of us; for if they had been of us they would no doubt have continued with us: but they went out that they might be made manifest that they were not of us." I John 2;18 -19

A man was an anti-Christ if he denied they Father and the Son. I John 2:22
He wrote the same thing in II John 7 "This is a deceiver and antichrist"
Peter warned of that same class of men. II Peter 2:1-2

1. There were false prophets among the people II Peter 2:1
   The people here means the people of Israel, God's chosen people.

2. There shall be false teachers among you.

   II Peter 2:1 Who privily shall bring in damnable heresies.

   Heresy means a choosing, hence opinion, but it's meaning here is a wrong opinion. False teachers have a wrong opinion of who Jesus is.

   They smuggle into the church false doctrine without the people knowing it. Jude says "certain men crept in unawares…ungodly men, turning the grace of our God into lasciviousness which is filthy words, unbridled lust and indecent bodily movements.

3. Denying the Lord that bought them. - Verse 1
Yet Christ has in a sense "bought" them also, for He died for all, including them that disown Him and bring upon themselves swift destruction. Their heresies of destruction bring upon themselves what their false teaching are bringing to others...eternal destruction.

"And many shall follow their pernicious ways. - Verse 2
The weak, simple minded and ignorant would be led astray.

The way of the truth shall be evil spoken of. - Verse 2
These false teachers were instructors in religion. But their doctrine denied Christ and their lives were unrestrained, lawless and immoral. How easy it was then for many to speak evil of the right way. God's people bring His word in freedom, boldness and without deceit, not so with a falsifier. He must be secretive and subtle. Since the year 1900 more than 1,100 claimed they were Christ. Matthew 24:5 says "many shall be deceived".

Satan is the great deceiver. He has:

1. False doctrines
2. False churches
3. False teachers
4. False preachers
5. False prophets
6. False Christs

Which will end with a certain person as the antichrist.

VERSE 6 REAL WARS AND RUMORS OF WARS

4. REAL WARS AND RUMORS OF WARS - Verse 6

Up until the turn of the century, wars were fought army against army. But now we mobilize whole nations and empires fight wars on a worldwide scale. There have been only 268 years of peace in the last 4,000 years of human history despite the signing of more than 8,000 peace treaties. War is a multi-billion dollar business. In Caesar's day, it took $.75 for a Roman soldier to kill the enemy. In World War I it had risen to $15,000, in World War II it had risen to $30,000, in the Korean War $50,000 and in the Vietnam War it had risen to $1,000,000. The Gulf War in Iraq carried a price tag of $4.3 billion per month shortly followed by the Afghan War at $800 million per month. Keep in mind wars will continue

15

and become more destructive and will end at the Battle of Armageddon Revelation 19:11-21.

World leaders keep warning everyone that the nations of the world are arming themselves at an alarming rate. It's not new, but these weapons of war are designed to kill. There is coming a day when there will be no more wars. "And He shall judge among the nations and shall rebuke many people: and they shall beat their swords into plowshares, and their spears into pruning hooks: Nation shall not lift up sword against nation, neither shall they learn war anymore" Isaiah 2:4.

VERSE 7 RACE WARS

5. **RACE WARS - Verse 7**
    a. **Race Wars**

> The word "nation" means race. Many races hate other races and go to war and millions have been killed.

    b. **Religious Wars**

> Like Cain, Islam is a religion of violence. - Genesis 4:1-8
> In Islamic wars multitudes slain. Hitler's war was religious and

racist and millions were killed. That Hitler was a god, no one could doubt. He was worshipped by millions and thought himself to be both infallible and indestructible. He hated the Jews with a passion and killed six million of them. God kept Israel as the apple of his eye - Deuteronomy 32:10.

"I will bless them that bless thee and curse him that curseth thee" - Genesis 12:3. "He who touches Israel for ill, will not go unpunished". Nations & individuals have proven this true of scripture. "He who touches Israel for good will be rewarded" - Matthew 25:40

c. Famines

The dark shadow of famine already casts itself heavily on the world. But according to the Lord's words of forecast. Things will get worse. Today half the world goes to bed hungry. Malnutrition already stalks the face of the globe and death from starvation takes 10,000 lives every day. Across the world famines are common and increasing. America has been blessed abundantly. Do we every look up and thank God for all that He has blessed us with? He has blessed us with:

Spiritual Blessings
1. His Gospel
        Good News
2. His Salvation
        Deliverance
3. Holy Spirit
        Comfort
4. His Death on the Cross   For sin
5. His Word to light our path

Temporal Blessings
1. Our Food
2. Our Raiment we wear
3. Our Family
4. Our Houses we live in
5. Our Cars we drive
6. Our Health
7. Our Freedom we have

We stand to lose all these things if America does not repent and turn back to God. Do not take these for granted.

d. Pestilences

Means deadly infectious disease.

Gone are the days when we thought that the medical field was going to solve and eliminate disease. Terrible new viruses have appeared. AIDS surfaced in the 1980's, it was restricted to male homosexuals, drug abusers and Haitians. Now millions are infected with HIV which causes the disease. Other viruses now known to exist in the hot zones and equatorial jungles of the earth. One of these viruses is Ebola, which dissolves the victim's internal organs and has no known cure.

e. Earthquakes in divers places

Earthquakes, for example, are greatly on the increase. Scientists who study earthquakes of the United States Geographical Survey have recorded 1976 as the year in which earthquake activity around the world took on new significance. Some interesting earthquake statistics show that the quakes have not only increased in intensity but they have also increased in frequency, which is shown by the following numerical statistics of quakes that registered over 6 on the Richter Scale during the listed decades.

Decade	Number of quakes over 6
1880 – 1890	1
1890 – 1900	1
1900 – 1910	3
1910 – 1920	2
1920 – 1930	2
1930 – 1940	5
1940 – 1950	4
1950 – 1960	9
1960 – 1970	13
1970 – 1980	46
1980 – 1990	52

In the 1990's earthquakes occurred even more often. Of the thirteen most devastating earthquakes ever to have occurred, ten of them occurred in the 20th century. The earthquake that will really cause the earth to topple on its axis will come at the time of the Battle of Armageddon. The most violent earthquake in all human history is described in Revelation 16:18.

VERSE 4-14 RANK OF ORDER

6. RANK OF ORDER - Verse 4-14

The word sorrow means birth pangs, labor pains, travailings, intolerable

20

anguish, quick, sharp, violent travailing pain.

A prelude of sorrow that is to follow during the Tribulation:

False Christs	Verses 4-5
Pestilence	Verse 7
Earthquakes	Verse 7
Martyrdoms	Verses 8-10
False Prophets	Verse 11
Increasing Lawlessness	Verse 12

All these sorrows are considered to be the beginning of birth pangs - Verse 8. As in childbirth, such agonies will be followed by much more severe pains before deliverance occurs. So will it be with the return of Christ in glory.

Coming events are casting their foreshadows. Note many of these signs, of course, have taken place throughout the church age in a lesser degree and will doubtless continue right up to the Rapture. They will occur in a greater degree after the Rapture of the church. The signs in verses 4-14 are the first 3 ½ years of the Tribulation period. These signs are happening today in a lesser degree. Matthew 24:15 begins the last 3 ½ years of the Tribulation. This is the 70th week of Daniel - Daniel 9:27. The

weeks are seven years. - Genesis
29:20-28. The seven years begins after
the church has been caught up to
heaven - I Thessalonians 4:17

VERSES *9-12* DISTRESS

7. *DISTRESS* - *Verses 9-12*

a. A TIME OF AFFLICTION, MARTYRDOM, HATE - Verse 9

Afflicted means anguish,
persecution, tribulation, trouble
For the Jew, this is the time of
Jacob's trouble - Jeremiah 30:7.

Martyrdom means to kill outright,
to destroy.
"They will put you out of the
synagogues; yea the time cometh,
that whosoever killeth you will
think that he doeth God service" -
John 16:2.
There were 3 degrees of
excommunication, or putting out of
the synagogue, among the Jews:
John 16:2

1. To be put out of the
synagogue meant isolation
from the social life in Israel.
2. It meant loss of
employment.

3. And rejection by their own family.

Behind all persecutions stands the liar and murderer from the beginning, that is the Devil. The future will bring another fulfillment of the words of our Lord for during the coming Great Tribulation, many Jews who have believed on Jesus as their Saviour, their coming King, will be martyred. The events described in these verses refer primarily to Israel and the Jews. During the Tribulation period, the nations will hate Israel and lay siege to Jerusalem.

I believe these predictions will have a double fulfillment. During the present age of grace, (in a lesser degree) and in the coming period of the Tribulation (in a greater degree) while the primary interpretation of this verse is applied to the Jew, it may be applied secondarily to Christians today. The person who lives a dedicated, Holy Spirit filled life, separated from the world will be hated by the world. Jesus said "If the world hate you, ye know that it hated me before it hated you" - John 15:18.

b. A TIME OF OFFENDING, BETRAYAL, HATE - Verse 10

i. **Offend** means to entrap, entice to sin, to fall away, to stumble, to make indignant.

The many who will be offended in anger will turn away from following Jesus. When persecutions come, they will not be willing to pay the price to walk with Him. They shall make shipwreck of faith, they have never known Jesus as Saviour.

ii. **Betray** means to surrender, deliver.
Deliver to an enemy by treachery. This is what Judas did to Christ, because of his inner hatred of Him, betrayed Him to His enemies. Family members betray each other - Mark 13:12 During the Tribulation unbelievers will viciously betray God's people.

iii. **Hate** means pursue with hatred, detest, despise.

In the last days there will be people that are despisers of

24

those that are good - II
Timothy 3:3. Sometimes
people are put off by a
Christian's sheer goodness.
The mere sight of them
becomes a rebuke to their
ungodliness.

VERSE 11 A TIME OF DECEPTION

c. A TIME OF DECEPTION - Verse 11

Jesus added the prediction that
many false prophets will arise to
join the numerous false Christ's -
Matthew 24:4-5. In a consolidated
attempt to deceive the people of
the world about the true Christ
and lead astray with their false
doctrines. Not long ago I read an
article that said many evangelical
churches had come to the
conclusion that there are many
ways to God other than Jesus.
Not so! Jesus is the only way to
God.

1. I am the way
2. The truth
3. The life
4. No man cometh to the
   Father but by me - John
   14:6

25

5. The only Saving Name - Acts 4:12
6. The only Door - John 10:9
7. The only Mediator – I Timothy 2:5

VERSE 12 A TIME OF ABOUNDING INIQUITY

d. A TIME OF ABOUNDING INIQUITY - Verse 12

1. **Iniquity** means lawlessness. It carries with it the idea of deliberately disobeying a specific standard. God's standard will be ignored. This will happen when the anti-Christ rules - II Thessalonians 2:3-4. Multitudes today are ignoring God's standard, His word. They pay no attention when it is preached or taught. They refuse to consider. Long ago Moses cried "O that they were wise, that they understood this, they would consider their latter end" - Deuteronomy 32:29.

- It reminds us of its certainty - Hebrews 9:27

"...it is appointed unto men once to die"

26

- Urges Preparation - Amos 4:12

  "Prepare to meet thy God.

- Warning to be ready - Matthew 24:44

  "...for in such an hour as ye think not, the Son of Man cometh"

2. **Abound** means to increase, be multiplied.

   It will be a time of unbridled lust when men will be engulfed in a tidal wave of wickedness and they will glory in it. Without the restraining power of the Holy Spirit at work, - II Thessalonians 2:7, men will wholeheartedly engage in every kind of conceivable sin

The forces of anarchy are already running rampant in the world.

27

MATTHEW 24: THE GATHERING STORM

1. The Home Has Waxed Cold

A. Love between husband and wife has waxed cold.

B. Love between children and parents has waxed cold.

C. Love between brothers and sisters has waxed cold.

D. Love between friends has waxed cold

E. Love of church has waxed cold

Thousands of churches have waxed cold toward God and His Word. They have a form of godliness but denying the power thereof - II Timothy 3:5. For by growing cold we are not to understand the lukewarm state, but an entirely lapsed condition; the fire is not merely cooled, but gone out.

VERSES 13-14 A TIME OF ENDURANCE AND PREACHING

e. **A TIME OF ENDURANCE AND PREACHING** - Verses 13-14

1. **Endure** means to remain i.e. abide, not recede or flee, to continue to be i.e. not perish, to last.

   I believe that this is a physical salvation. The Tribulation saints who endure (survive) to the end of the Tribulation (when Jesus comes) will be delivered (saved) from physical death. They will enter into the millennial kingdom in their human bodies. This will be true for those saints who do manage to survive the destruction of the Tribulation. Many will not survive, but will be martyred for their faith in Jesus - Revelation 13:15.

2. **Preaching**

   a. *The Gospel of the Grace of God*

29

During the present age, the gospel preached is of the grace of God - Acts 20:24 - His death to put away sin and His resurrection to justify the believer, and the incorporation of all believers into a body (the church) of which Christ is the head. It is called the gospel of Jesus Christ - Mark 1:1. The gospel of God - Romans 1:1. The Gentiles, also Jews are included.

b. *The Preaching of the Kingdom - Verse 14*

The gospel of the kingdom was the message preached by both John the Baptist and Jesus when they proclaimed, "Repent ye for the kingdom of heaven is at hand" - Matthew 3:2 - Matthew 4:17. It had both a salvation message (repent) and an end-time emphasis. The main focus of the gospel of the kingdom is the announcement that the kingdom (millennial) is at hand; it is near. The gospel of the kingdom will be preached during the Tribulation. John and Jesus were calling Israel to repentance to an acknowledgement of their sinful condition and their need of salvation. After Israel rejected their Messiah (Christ), the gospel of the kingdom was not again proclaimed because the kingdom had to be postponed. However, during the Tribulation when the Lord will again deal with Israel (the church will be in heaven), the gospel of the kingdom will once again be preached.

Those Who Proclaim It

The 144,000 witnesses - Revelation 7:1-8 and the two mighty witnesses - Revelation 11:3-12 will announce the "good news" that the "Messiah's" return is at hand, at which time He will establish His messianic kingdom. Also the gospel of the kingdom will offer salvation by grace through based upon (as always) the shed blood and death of Jesus Christ. The results are a great multitude that no man could number, of all nations, kindred's, peoples, tongues stood before the throne and before the Lamb clothed with white robes and palms in their hands - Revelation 7:8 "These are they which came out of great tribulation and have washed their robes and made them white in the blood of the Lamb" - Revelation 7:14.

3. **The Everlasting Gospel - Revelation 14:6-7**

God has used various means to communicate the gospel to the people of the world. During the church age in which we are now living, the gospel is committed to men or the church itself to give to the world - II Corinthians 5:18 "And all things are of God, who hath reconciled us to Himself by Jesus Christ and hath given to us the ministry of reconciliation". During the first 3 ½ years of the Tribulation, the two witnesses of Revelation 11 will be given power to preach the gospel.

32

But in Revelation 14:6-7, It is an angel who preaches the gospel. At first this may appear to be a new means by which God spreads abroad the gospel, but is it new? At other times, especially in the Old Testament, angels have been used of God to declare His message. Hebrews 2:2 tells us that "the word spoken by angels was steadfast". During the extremely difficult time of the Great Tribulation (the last 3 ½ years), an angel will be used to proclaim the gospel. Angels are indestructible, therefore, no matter how intense the persecution becomes, it will not affect them. God is never left without a witness. This is the ageless gospel that has never changed, and is also a message of judgment, "for the hour of his judgment is come."

VERSE 15 DANIEL'S PROPHECY

8. DANIEL'S PROPHECY - Verse 15
a. Historic

This is a reference to Daniel 9:27, 11:31. There is both a historic and prophetic reference here. During the time of the Greek conquest of Israel under Antiochus Epiphanes, a pig was sacrificed upon the altar of the restored temple thus desecrating it and to the Jews, this was an Abomination of Desolation. Antiochus Epiphanes was a type of the anti-Christ who will sit in the temple and call himself God - II Thessalonians 2:4 and the pig was an unclean animal.

b. Prophetic

The anti-Christ will make a covenant with the Jews in the first 3 ½ years of the Tribulation to protect them from their enemies - Daniel 9:27. In the midst of the seven years, he will break the covenant and cause the sacrifice in the restored temple to cease and desecrate the temple and he will claim to be God and demand to be worshipped as God - II Thessalonians 2:4.

Read Revelation 13:14-15

Abomination means impure, hateful, to stink.

The word has connection with spiritual, idolatry - Revelation chapters 17 & 18 and perpetrators of an abomination will find no place in the new Jerusalem - Revelation 21:7. All false religions stink in the nostrils of God.

VERSES 16-22 DAY OF WRATH

9. DAY OF WRATH - Verses 16-22

Then when the anti-Christ enters Judea and takes over the temple - Daniel 9:27; 11:40-45 Israel will have to flee Judea. Many scholars believe the ultimate place of hiding for these refugees will be the ancient rock city of Petra. Petra is located about 50 miles south of the Dead Sea in the mountain country of Edom, now in present day Transjordan. The city and tombs are almost all cut unto the rock cliffs of the mountains and its principal entrance was through the narrow twisting gorge between cliffs towering 500 feet high. Years ago W. E. Blackstone, author of the book "Jesus Is Coming", was so convinced that Petra will be the place in which the Jews are kept safe during the last 3 ½ years of the Great Tribulation, he purchased thousands of Hebrew New Testaments, underlined passages like Matthew 24 and Revelation 12, and left them in earthen jars throughout Petra. When the Jews get there, the Bibles will be awaiting them. Some scholars believe God may also have other secret areas around the Dead Sea and in the mountains of Moab and Edom. God knows and has it all planned. I quote Dr. Rod Mattoon in his book "Luke Volume 5",Chapter 21:5-20, Page 287. "How big does the place of refuge need to be? We do know that all the Jews will not escape; only a remnant will remain after two-thirds of the Jews have been killed - Zechariah 13:8-9. The present Jewish population is approximately 13 million. If that figure stays consistent, the hiding place will need to hold at least 4.5 million people. In Petra some caves have a capacity of up to 3,000 people. Guides in Petra have stated that this area could easily hold five million people.

Daniel Chapter 11:41 tells us that Edom, Moab and Ammon will escape the hand of the anti-Christ. Ammon is east of the Jordan river. Moab is east of the Dead Sea. Edom is 50 miles south of the Dead Sea. This region now is Transjordan. "Edom and Moab and the chief of the children of Ammon". (According to Isaiah 11:14 these three nations will be conquered at the return of Christ by the remnant of Israel).

VERSES 15-20 Warning

a. Warning - Verses 15-20

There is a warning to flee "the Abomination of Desolation" - Verse 16 (the anti-Christ) immediately. No believers will be able to stand against anti-Christ, not even the strongest. The imminent danger and urgency is stressed by Christ in 4 statements.

Verse 17 A PERSON IS TO FORGET ALL COMFORT OF HOME

i. *A Person is to Forget All Comfort of Home - Verse 17*

In ancient days the rooftops of houses were left flat; they were used for rest, meditation, and neighborly visits. Most houses had steps both inside and outside that led up to the roof. When the abomination (the anti-Christ in the restored temple) is seen, the danger is so imminent that a person should flee from his roof immediately using the outside stairs.

VERSE 18 A PERSON IS TO FORGET ALL PERSONAL POSSESSIONS

ii. *A Person is to Forget All Personal Possessions - Verse 18*

Not return from work to get his clothes (or possessions).

VERSE 19 A PERSON IS TO GRIEVE FOR THOSE WHO CANNOT FLEE RAPIDLY

iii. *A Person is to Grieve for Those Who Cannot Flee Rapidly - Verse 19*

Especially pregnant women who are responsible for small children. Many dear mothers worry about this verse. Be assured mothers and mothers-to-be, if you carry an unborn child, you have nothing to worry about, because when this comes to pass all the saved will be with Jesus in heaven. This has to do with Jewish mothers during the Tribulation period. It will be a time of sorrow and woe to mothers and expectant mothers in Israel. But it does not refer to any mother at the present time who is born again. The mother with small children could not travel as rapidly as those who have no children to take with them. The expectant mothers could not walk as rapidly as those who are not

with child. A time of grief,
distress, deep suffering.

VERSE 20 A PERSON IS TO PRAY FOR GOOD CONDITIONS IN FLEEING

iv. *A Person is to Pray For Good Conditions in Fleeing - Verse 20*

Pictured by both Winter and the Sabbath Day.

1. Winter

Not in Winter: for then the days would be short, and the difficulty of finding sustenance increase. No fruit bearing on trees, or in the fields. Beside their inability to lodge in the inclement open air. So they were to pray that it would not be in the Winter.

2. Sabbath Day

Neither on the Sabbath Day: The distance a Jew could travel on the Sabbath without breaking the law. The phrase occurs in Acts 1:12 where Mount Olivet is described as being "near

Jerusalem a Sabbath Day's journey". The distance is usually about a thousand yards. The orthodox Jews hold it unlawful to travel more than a mile on that day. "Neither on the Sabbath Day", a reference to the difficulty of travel (securing lodging, meals, services) on the Sabbath in an area where orthodox Legalist Jews will be observing such restrictions. The Sabbath was Jewish institution which was not binding on Christian believers.

VERSES 21-22 GREAT TRIBULATION

GREAT TRIBULATION - Verses 21-22

The last 3 ½ years of the Tribulation period will be a time of unprecedented horror and holocaust on earth. And the only chance of escape you will be to take the warning of Jesus Christ seriously enough to obey them. The ferocity of those days will be unlike any other time in human history -

Daniel 12:1 "...except those days should be shortened, there should no flesh be saved" - Verse 22. It is clear from the books of Daniel and Revelation that the final period of the Tribulation is exactly 1,260 days or 42 months, both of which are 3 ½ years. Daniel 12:7 - the time and times and a half is 3 ½ years. Revelation 13:5-6 - The anti-christ's blasphemy against God and the length of his reign is 42 months - Verse 5. Does God mean that He will shorten the Great Tribulation to fewer than 1,260 days? No, to shorten the days means that He limits them to 3 ½ years. Mark's record of Jesus' same statement sheds light on its meaning - Mark 13:20. Two things should be noted about Jesus' statement:

1. **First,** in the ancient world the verb that is consistently translated "shortened" in the Matthew and Mark passage primarily meant "To cut off". It frequently was used to refer to the

cutting off of hands and feet.

2. **Second**, the two verbs translated "had shortened" and "hath shortened" in the Mark passage and the verb translated "should be shortened" in the Matthew passage - Matthew 24:22 are all in the aorist tense which means to put this action in the past. I am not saying the Great Tribulation has already past, I am saying the decision to shorten the days of the Great Tribulation was made in the past eternity by God.

THE TIME OF SHORTENING

When in the past did God shorten the Great Tribulation? Jesus' statement about the shortening in Mark 13:20 clearly indicates that God shortened it sometime before Jesus made His statement. God decreed or determined what will happen during the course of world history:

43

Isaiah 14:24-27; 46:9-11; Daniel 9:24-27; 11:36; Luke 22:22; Acts 2:23; 4:27-28

Ephesians 1:11; 3:11

What God has determined cannot be annulled - Isaiah 14:24-27

In the light of what has been seen, we can conclude that in eternity past God shortened the Great Tribulation in the sense that He decreed or determined to cut it off at a specific time rather than to let it continue indefinitely. God sovereignly fixed a specific time for the Great Tribulation to end when it had run its course, 3 ½ years or 42 months or 1,260 days.

The strong figurative statement "cut off", "amputated", "mutilated" indicates that God has forcefully acted not to permit them to extend to full length that human passions would have carried them. No flesh denotes human life in its frailty and infirmity. God has curtailed the period to prevent the destruction of the human race.

VERSES 23-26 DECEPTION

10. DECEPTION - Verses 23-26

Their Performance - Verses 23-24

Feigned Report - Verse 23

"...Lo here is Christ, or there, believe it not."

Fake Christs - Verse 24

Many claim to be Christ. Jim Jones – Father Divine

False Prophets - **Verse 24**

Shall shew great signs and wonders.

Jesus forewarned them - Verse 25-26

"...if they shall say unto you, behold he is in the desert: go not forth: behold he is in the secret chambers: believe it not."

In the midst of all these trials false Christ's and false prophets will arise, no doubt promising to solve the problems or meet the needs of the hour. As credentials, they show "signs and wonders", either fabricating amazing things or by demonic power

45

actually performing miracles. Supernatural demonstrations do not prove that a ministry is of God.

Signs appeal to the understanding, wonders appeal to the imagination.

These false Christ's and prophets will be so clever in fact, that Jesus said "…if it were possible they (would even) deceive the very elect (the saved)" - Matthew 24:24. It is obvious, however, from the fact that the Lord used the words, "**IF** possible": that the anti-Christ's deceptive co-laborers will not be successful in deceiving the elect. Satan has never been able to deceive born again Christians about the identity of the Lord. Why? Jesus said "My sheep hear my voice and I know them" - John 10:27.

VERSES 27-30 DESTRUCTION

11. DESTRUCTION - Verses 27-30

a. SWIFTNESS OF CHRIST'S SECOND COMING - Verse 27

Like lightening, swift, sudden, unexpected, unannounced, global, visible.

"Every eye shall see Him"
Revelation 1:7

VERSE 28 SUPPER OF THE GREAT GOD–ARMAGEDDON

b. SUPPER OF THE GREAT GOD– ARMAGEDDON–Verse 28– Revelation 19:17

Many birds are predatory in their eating habits. It would appear that all kinds of birds will come to feed on the carrion of the Great Battle. Eagles can also find corpses on which to feed themselves and their young because God made them that way. The eagles of Palestine eat dead bodies, that is clear from Job 39:27, Proverbs 30:17 and Revelation 19:17. Other birds of prey, many species of hawks, eagles and vultures are found in the Holy Land, also will be there. Armageddon means "mount of slaughter". God prepares a supper of grief, ghastly and gloom which stands in sharp contrast to the gladness and joy of the Marriage Supper of the Lamb.

i. The Supper of Delight - Revelation 19:9

The Marriage Supper of the Lamb

47

    ii.   **The Supper of Destruction - Revelation 19:17-18**

Armageddon, where the slain are there is she - Job 39:30 i.e. on the field of battle.

VERSE 29 SOLAR SYSTEM DARKENS

    c. **SOLAR SYSTEM DARKENS - Verse 29**

The events mentioned here clearly were not fulfilled at Pentecost. There is no conflict here between Joel 2:31 and Acts 2:20. Joel tells of the darkening of the sun and the moon into blood.

Before the great and notable Day of the Lord.

Matthew 24:29 tells us immediately **After** the Tribulation of those days "...shall the sun be darkened, and the moon shall not give her light, and the stars shall fall from heaven, and the powers of the heavens shall be shaken."

These events will take place immediately prior to the return of Jesus Christ at the middle and end of the Tribulation. Note - See Matthew 24:27-33; Revelation 6:12, 8:7-12, 16:10. "The powers of the heavens shall be shaken": the heavens need to be cleansed so as to prepare a passage through which the descending Son of Man may pass through.

VERSE 30 THE SIGN

d. THE SIGN - Verse 30

The grandeur of Jesus Christ appearing in the sky visible for all to see, no doubt, will be a powerful **SIGN** to an unbelieving world. Moreover, every eye shall see Him as He comes in the clouds with power and great glory. See Revelation 1:7. The Lord's return will have opposite effects **Upon His Foes - Verse 30.** Defeating the world's assembled military forces at Armageddon. Many of the people of the world will evidently mourn in fear of Him. **And His Friends - Verse 31** sadness and gladness, waling and worship, dread and delight. Jesus will not come at the end as He did in the beginning, in weakness and humbly, but with power and great glory.

VERSE 31 THE SENDING FORTH OF HIS ANGELS

e. THE SENDING FORTH OF HIS ANGELS - Verse 31

Angels will be sent forth with a might trumpet blast to gather His people of Israel from the farthest ends of the earth. Then, now, and even in Jesus' day, Jews were scattered to the four winds (direction) of the earth. Though there has been a limited regathering of Israel to the land even in this generation, the present return of Jews is in unbelief. Then it will be all together and in belief. Note - Isaiah 43:5-7; Jeremiah 16:14-16, 23:3; Deuteronomy 30:1-6.

VERSES 32-41 DESCRIPTION

12. DESCRIPTION - Verses 32-41

a. PARABLE OF THE FIG TREE - Verses 32-33

Israel has often been symbolized in Scripture as a fig tree. The fig tree

illustrating the nearness of His return. By December, the fig trees of Israel have shed their leaves, and they remain bare to the close of March. Suddenly, the leaf buds appear signifying the arrival of Spring. The signs "these things" (Verse 33) are the items previously mentioned that the end is near.
Old Testament

Jeremiah 24, Ezekiel 37, Joel 1:6-7, Hosea 9:10

New Testament

Matthew 24:32, Luke 13:6-9

VERSES 34-35 PRESERVATION

b. **PRESERVATION - Verses 34-35**

i. *OF ISRAEL - Verse 34*

This generation (means family, race). Israel will not disappear before the prophetic word has been fulfilled

ii. *OF THE BIBLE - Verse 35*

"Heaven and earth shall pass away, but My word shall not pass away."

GOD'S WORD

- **IT'S PLAN** - **Verse 34**

  "Till all these things be fulfilled".

- **IT'S PERMANENCE Verse 35**

  "Shall not pass away"

- **IT'S POWER Hebrews 4:12**

1. Quick   -   Alive
2. Powerful   -   Energy
3. Sharper   -   To Cut
4. Piercing   -   To Penetrate
5. Discerner   -   Penetrate into the depth of the soul

iii. *ALSO MEANS:*

That generation living at that time of whatever race they may be.

VERSE 36 PROVIDENCE OF GOD

c. **PROVIDENCE OF GOD - Verse 36**

Having told His disciples to watch for the signs of His return, Jesus saw the need to warn them about date setting. They could see the signs, but guessing the day or the hour of His return was foolish.

In Mark 13:32, Jesus said He did not know at that time (when He spoke the discourse) the precise day and hour of His return. He willingly limited himself in certain capacities during His incarnation

Jesus was fully God as well as fully man, yet he voluntarily restricted His use of certain divine attributes when He took up temporary residence in a human body. Philippians 2:7 "But made Himself of no reputation, and took upon Him the form of a servant, and was made in the likeness of men". The word "reputation" means to empty. Jesus did not empty Himself of His deity or being God. He did not lose His divine attributes. He merely lad them aside willingly and did not use them or manifest them except as He was directed by His Father – John 4:34. The existence of all knowledge and limited knowledge in one and the same person is part of the mystery of the incarnation of the divine and the human in one personality - I Timothy 3:16.

Deuteronomy 33:27   He is the Eternal God

Isaiah 9:6   He is the Everlasting Father

Since Christ is risen from the dead and is glorified, He speaks with certainty in Revelation 22:20 "I come quickly". Christ now fully knows the time of His return.

VERSES 37-39 POINT OF LIKENESS

d. **POINT OF LIKENESS - Verses 37-39**

DAYS OF NOAH

i. SINFUL

"Imagination of the thoughts of his heart was only evil continually" - Genesis 6:5.

54

ii.   SERIOUS

No one took Noah seriously, except his immediate family.

iii.   SUDDEN JUDGMENT

"He that being often reproved hardeneth his neck, shall suddenly be destroyed and that without remedy" - Proverbs 29:1

iv.   INDIFFERENCE - Verse 38
The affairs of everyday life. They were eating, drinking, marrying and giving in marriage,... until the day Noah entered the ark.

VERSE 39 IGNORANCE

v.   IGNORANCE - Verse 39

"**And knew not** until the flood came and took all away..."

In the days of Noah people ignored God and carried on with their lives as they always did. So, too, people now go about business as usual, some say I have heard that all of my life and He (Jesus) has not come yet. Others say I do not want to hear that it makes me nervous; still others say we don't need that kind of preaching. II Peter 3:3-7 tells about scoffers "knowing this first that shall in the last days scoffers walking after their own lusts, and saying where is the promise of His coming, for since the fathers fell asleep (died), all things continue as they were from the beginning of creation". "For this they are willingly ignorant of that by the Word of God, the heavens were of old, and the earth standing out of the water and in the water: whereby the world that then was, being overflowed with water, perished. But the heavens and the earth, which are now, by the same word are kept in store, reserved unto fire

THE END OF THE WORLD, THE COURSE OF THE AGE

against the day of judgment and perdition of ungodly men".

VERSE 40-41 INDIGNATION

vi.   INDIGNATION - Verse 40-41

As the people in the days of Noah were taken away in the judgment of the flood, so will many people be taken away in the destructive calamities of the Tribulation period, especially during the last 3 ½ years called the Great Tribulation. In this illustration Jesus cited: "two in the field; one taken the other left" "two women grinding at the mill; one taken the other left" also in Luke 17:30-37. In Luke 17:30-37 the context clearly is Armageddon which immediately precedes the coming of Christ in power and glory.

VERSES 42-44 DILIGENCE

13.DILIGENCE - Verses 42-44

a. **WATCHFULNESS - Verses 42-43**

A. Of keeping awake
B. Of spirit alertness
C. Be watchful
D. Be vigilant

b. **WARNING - Verse 44**

Since no one knows for certain when a thief might strike, he needs to be on guard at all times; likewise believers need to be watching always for the coming of Jesus.

14. *DIVINE STEWARDSHIP - Verses 45-51*

VERSES 45-47 THE FAITHFUL SERVANT

i. **THE FAITHFUL SERVANT - Verses 45-47**

His responsibility: He is to oversee his Master's household and to feed his Master's family. Feed the flock of God I Peter 5:2-3. He is to provide food for God's family in due season. He gives food at the right time. "Blessed is that servant whom his Lord when he cometh shall find doing, for his faithfulness the Lord will reward him at His return."

VERSE 48-51 THE EVIL SERVANT

ii. THE EVIL SERVANT - Verse 48-51

- *DENIAL - Verse 48*

  The evil servant denies the second coming of Christ. Doubting God's word that He is ever coming. Ignoring the Lord's coming in order to allow the person to live as he wishes. He says "And saying, where is the promise of His coming? For since the fathers fell asleep (died), all things continue as they were from the beginning of creation. For they are willingly ignorant of that by the word of God" - II Peter 3:4-5.

VERSES 49 DISREGARD FOR HIS FELLOW SERVANTS

- *DISREGARD FOR HIS FELLOWSERVANTS - Verses 49*

  1. CARELESSNESS - Verse 49

     He is saying something "in his heart", that is to himself. Now what a man says to himself is often even more important than what he says openly. See Proverbs 23:7; Matthew 9:3-21; Luke 12:17; 15:17 - 19. But within the precincts of his own being, this particular man is considering wickedly, irresponsibly.

  2. CRUELTY - Verse 49

     Smite his fellow servants

     The evil servant proved he was not really saved

because he took advantage of his Master's absence to beat his fellow man.

3. CAROUSING - Verse 49

    To eat and drink with the drunkards, those who scoff at the return of Christ, do not behave themselves well. "There shall come in the last days scoffers walking after their own lusts". They are cruel and carousers.

VERSE 50 DISTRACTED

- *DISTRACTED - Verse 50*

    The evil servant mind was drawn away in another direction. Those who are unprepared will not be looking for Jesus when He returns. Remember Lot's wife, she looked back toward Sodom and turned into a pillar of salt - Genesis 19:26. The evil servant was not looking for his Master's return and not even aware of His return.

VERSE 51 DESTRUCTION

- *DESTRUCTION - Verse 51*

  This weeping is that of inconsolable, never ending, wretchedness and utter, everlasting hopelessness. The accompanying gnashing of teeth denotes excruciating pain and frenzied anger. The one sin that damns sinners is the sin of omission. They failed to take Him (Jesus) into account. That, ultimately, is what sends people to Hell.

INDEX OF WORDS AND PHRASES

ABOUT THE AUTHOR

Guy Lee was born April 10, 1929. He accepted the Lord Jesus Christ as his personal Savior in August 1945 at the age of 16. After he was saved, the Lord called him into the ministry to preach and teach God's Word in 1950.

Guy is widely known for his knowledge and teaching of the Bible. He is one of the most respected Bible teachers in the northeast Georgia area. He has helped many young preachers get a head start in their ministry by praying for them and providing them with good sound doctrinal study resources.

The desire of Guy's heart is to see lost souls saved and grow in the grace and knowledge of the Lord. He hopes that the information and materials in this book will be used to accomplish just that.

Guy holds an Honorary Doctor of Divinity Degree from the Bethany Divinity College and Seminary in Dothan, Alabama. He was a circuit-riding Preacher, Pastor, Evangelist, and is now a 91 y/o who has written multiple Biblical sound works such as Daniel, Jude, Matthew, etc., etc., with the most excellent alliteration and thorough exegesis.